M is for Maple Syrup

A Vermont Alphabet

Written by Cynthia Furlong Reynolds
Illustrated by Ginny Joyner

Up where the north wind blows just a little keener,
up where the grasses grow just a little greener,
up where the mountain peaks rise a little higher,
up where the human kind draws just a little nigher,
that's where Vermont comes in.

CHARLES HIAL DARLING

Sleeping Bear Press
310 North Main Street
P.O. Box 20
Chelsea, MI 48118
www.sleepingbearpress.com
1-800-487-2323

Printed and bound in Canada.

10 9 8 7 6 5 4 3 2 1

Library of Congress Cataloging-in-Publication Data
Reynolds, Cynthia Furlong.
M is for maple syrup: A Vermont alphabet / by Cynthia Furlong Reynolds,
illustrated by Ginny Joyner
p.cm.
Summary: People, places, animals, and characteristic things of Vermont
are represented by the letters of the alphabet, with information about
them presented in rhyme and explanatory notes.
ISBN: 1-58536-030-9
Vermont—Juvenile literature. 2. English language—Alphabet—Juvenile literature. [1.
Vermont. 2. Alphabet.] I. Joyner, Ginny, ill. II. Title.

F49.3 .R49 2002
974.3—dc21   2002021700

F is for Family and Friends:

To my husband, my children,
and the Stanleys of Franklin and South Burlington, Vermont,

and to friends all around the country
who have encouraged me through the years.

My love, and many thanks!

CINDY

L is for my daughter Lucie,
my biggest fan and a great artist herself.

C is for Charlie,
an angel in wolf's clothing.

And F is for my big family,
who will probably buy lots of copies of this book.

GINNY

In 1789, Vermont schoolteacher Justin Morgan received a colt as payment for a debt. Little did he know that he would get far more than he bargained for! That stallion died at the age of 29 after launching America's only native line of horses. The Morgan is our state animal.

Known for their stamina, speed, and sweet dispositions, Morgans are out-standing saddle horses and equally good at pulling farm equipment. Their bodies are deep and short-backed, with thin legs and heads held high. When fully grown, they stand between 58 and 62 inches at the shoulders and weigh between 800 and 1,200 pounds. The Tennessee walking horse and American saddle horse are Morgan relatives.

You can see these horses at the University of Vermont's Morgan Horse Farm in Middlebury.

Alphabet and Animal begin with A.
Our state animal says neigh-neigh!
He wears four shoes and nibbles fresh green hay.
Watch him trot and gallop on a brilliant autumn day.

The covered bridge is a product of two important Yankee characteristics: ingenuity (which means imagination) and thrift (spending money wisely). The roofs protect the wooden supports and floors from decay; the sides carry the weight of the floor and roof. At one time, covered bridges were called "kissing bridges" because a man could steal a kiss from a lady in his carriage or sleigh when they passed through the bridge.

Vermont has 100 covered bridges, most of them still in use. The smallest are 40 feet long. The longest (crossing from Windsor to Cornish, New Hampshire) is 465 feet long. The oldest is Middlebury's Pulp Mill Bridge, built between 1808 and 1820. The newest appeared in Woodstock in 1981. The bridge at Wolcott is the only covered railroad bridge still used in our country today.

Bridge begins with the letter B.
Bridges cross rivers worry-free.
Don't close your eyes or you will miss
drivers on covered bridges stealing a kiss!

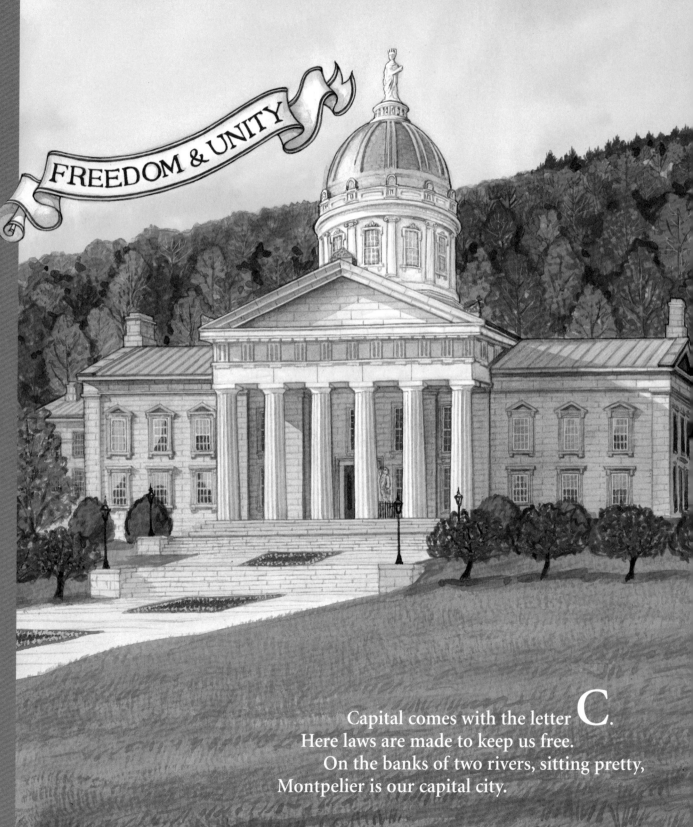

FREEDOM & UNITY

Our capital city, Montpelier, was settled on the Winooski and North Branch rivers in 1787.

During the American Revolution, Vermont was an independent republic, with its own laws, money, and government. In 1791, Vermont joined the Union as the 14th state. Montpelier became the capital in 1805.

Constitution is another important **C** word. A constitution is a set of laws that govern and protect the people. Vermont's constitution created a government with three parts: a governor, Supreme Court (with five judges called justices); and the General Assembly (which has two parts, with 30 senators and 150 representatives.) Our 1777 constitution was the first in the United States to outlaw slavery and give all adult males the right to vote.

Capital comes with the letter C.
Here laws are made to keep us free.
On the banks of two rivers, sitting pretty,
Montpelier is our capital city.

D is for Dairy,
a Vermont farm that is legendary.
Here, cows and goats are necessary
because making milk is customary.

Vermont's state drink is milk, which comes from the cows and goats raised on Vermont's dairy farms. One-quarter of Vermont's 6,900 farms are dairy farms; most of them lie in the river valleys up north. They produce more than two billion gallons of milk each year. Thanks to our dairy farmers, we have milk to drink and pour on our cereal, cheese for sandwiches, butter for bread, yogurt, cream, and, of course, mouth-watering ice cream.

Vermont farms provide milk for New England and cheese for sale all over the world. There are many dairy farms open to the public. One is Shelburne Farms, which sits on 1,400 acres outside Burlington.

d

D

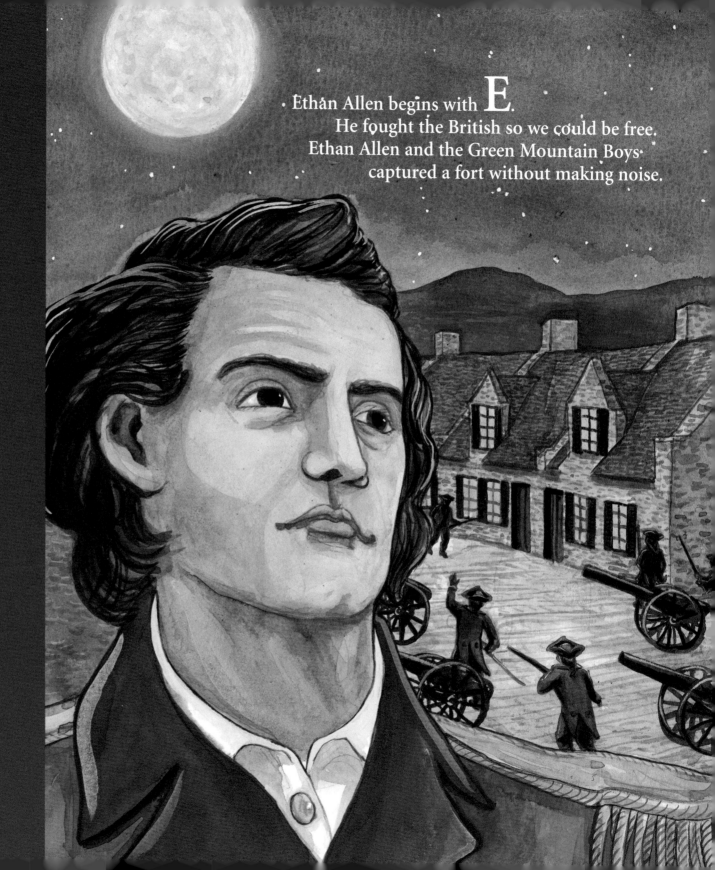

On May 10, 1775, Ethan Allen and his Green Mountain Boys surprised the British commander at Fort Ticonderoga while he and his troops were sleeping. Ethan Allen demanded the surrender of the fort overlooking Lake Champlain "in the name of the Great Jehovah and the Continental Congress." With the fort they captured cannons and mortars that were later sent to Boston where they were used for the Battle of Bunker Hill. These cannons and mortars played a big part in forcing the British to leave Boston Harbor.

Born in Litchfield, Connecticut in 1738, Ethan Allen became a legendary frontiersman. He moved to the New Hampshire Grants (now Vermont) in 1768 and, with his five brothers, joined a band of freedom fighters called the Green Mountain Boys. After capturing Fort Ticonderoga, Ethan Allen joined the American army. He wrote about his adventures in *A Narrative of Colonel Ethan Allen's Captivity*. He died in 1789, in Burlington. You can tour his home there.

Ethan Allen begins with E.
He fought the British so we could be free.
Ethan Allen and the Green Mountain Boys
captured a fort without making noise.

Ff

F is for Fish.
If you want to catch a fish,
  bait a line and make a wish.
    Trout and pike make a fine fish dish!

Fishermen have fun trying to catch the 20 kinds of edible fish that swim in Vermont's waters.

Vermont's state cold-water fish, the brook trout, plays hide-and-seek among rocks, logs, and the banks of icy streams and lakes. Their olive-green bodies have worm-like marks on their backs. Their sides are speckled with red spots inside blue halos. Their tail is nearly square, with orange fins. The males' bellies become bright orange in the fall, when females begin to lay their eggs.

A member of the perch family, the walleye pike is Vermont's state warm-water fish. Long, slim, and yellowish-brown, pike have large mouths, canine teeth, and two separate dorsal fins. Their heads and backs are darker than their sides, and their bellies are cream-colored. The walleye's long, thin, forked tails have a white patch. They feed on smaller fishes and tiny animals in deep waters.

G is for the mountains painted Green,
starring in many an artist's scene.
Buried in those mountains that you can see
are Garnet and Granite, which also start with G.

G g

Vermont owes its name and its nick-name—the Green Mountain State—to French explorer Samuel de Champlain. In 1609, when he first viewed Vermont's mountain ranges colored with the deep blue-greens of balsam, hemlock, and white pine trees, he christened the area Verd Monts or "les monts verts." Vert means "green" and mont means "mountain" in French.

The grossular garnet—a crystalized mineral formed by silica, aluminum and magnesium—is Vermont's state gem. Granite, a hard stone cut from the ground, is one of Vermont's three state rocks (the others are marble and slate).

G is also for Grandma Moses. Born Anna Mary Robertson in 1860, she was 76 when she began painting country scenes. Her schoolhouse and paintings can be seen at the Bennington Museum.

The state bird of Vermont is the hermit thrush. Many birdwatchers believe that the hermit thrush's music is the most beautiful of all birds' songs. It begins with one clear note, then the thrush sings on different pitches, which is unusual for a bird. When they want to sound a warning, they call *tuck...tuck.*

Up to 7½ inches long, the hermit thrush has a brown jacket, spotted brown chest, and rust-colored tail, which he loves to flick.

Thrushes eat buds in spring, berries and insects in summer. The mothers lay four to six blue-green eggs in cup-shaped nests made of moss, leaves, and tiny roots and hidden on the ground or in low bushes.

h
H

H is for the happy Hermit thrush,
brown, spotted, living in the underbrush.
This bird croons a lovely musical tune
while snacking on berries in the afternoon.

Vermont's dairy cows are responsible for the creamiest, dreamiest, most delectable frozen delicacies. Our state's favorite ice cream was developed by two ice cream lovers, Ben Cohen and Jerry Greenfield, who built a factory in Waterbury that makes dream-come-true ice cream flavors. Ben & Jerry's buys cream from nearly 600 Vermont dairy farms whose farmers promise to raise their cows the healthy, old-fashioned way.

Their ice cream flavors have names as creative as the delicious combinations of ingredients—not just fruits, nuts, fudge, marshmallows, and caramel, but also candies. When you tour the Waterbury factory, you can sample the newest flavors of ice creams and sorbets.

I i

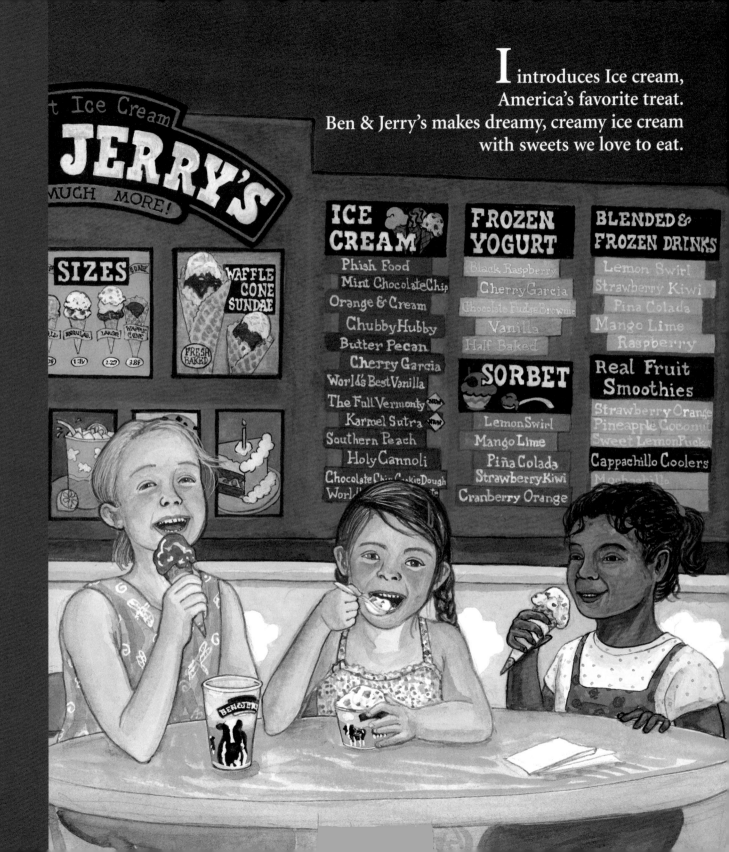

I introduces Ice cream,
America's favorite treat.
Ben & Jerry's makes dreamy, creamy ice cream
with sweets we love to eat.

Joke begins with the letter J.
A joke is something funny that people say.
Vermonters tell jokes with very straight faces
about themselves and tourists and other places.

Vermonters love their jokes—quiet jokes, which make people pause for a moment in the course of their day to think. A Vermont sense of humor has been described as a "dry wit," "wooden," and "straight-faced"—but if you look closely, you'll see a twinkle in the speaker's eye.

The classic Vermont joke runs something like this: A tourist walks up to a Vermont farmer and asks how to get to a nearby town. The farmer replies, "Oh, you can't get there from here."

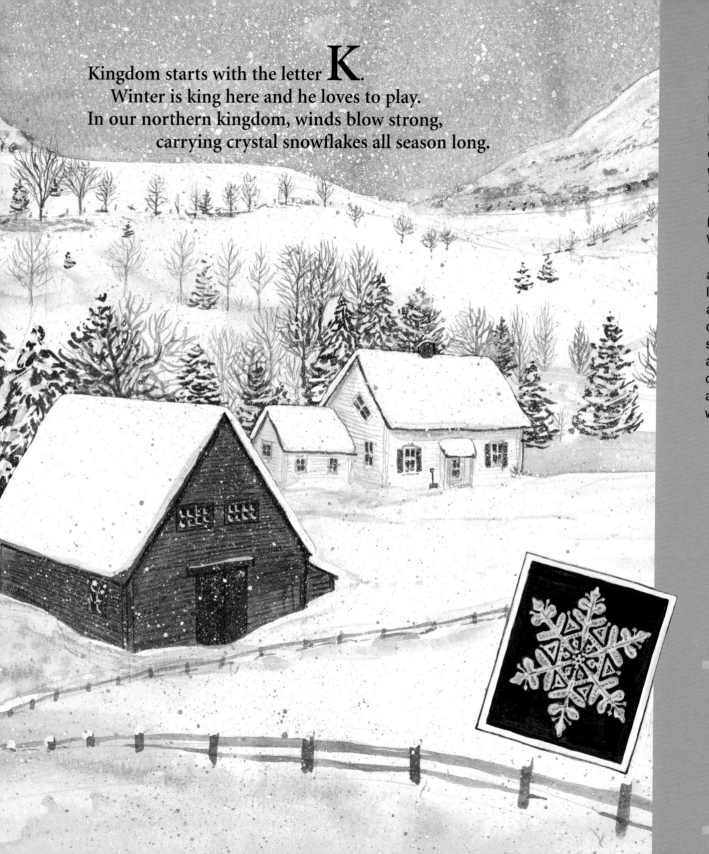

Kingdom starts with the letter K.
Winter is king here and he loves to play.
In our northern kingdom, winds blow strong,
carrying crystal snowflakes all season long.

When you head north as far as you can go in Vermont, you find a rugged, breathtakingly beautiful place that Vermonters call "The Kingdom." Bordered by Montgomery and Jay to the west, Newport and Derby to the east, this is our state's snowbelt. A winter's snowfall can total more than 30 feet here.

Born in Jericho, a farmer named Wilson "Snowflake" Bentley (1865-1926) dedicated his life to studying and photographing snowflakes. He learned that each snowflake begins as a speck too tiny to see. Then, tiny bits of water attach to the speck to form six branches. Wind and moisture affect the way that ice crystals grow on those branches. No two flakes are alike; all are beautiful hexagonal works of art.

On July 30, 1609, Samuel de Champlain stood at Chimney Point and bestowed his name on the huge body of water he saw.

The largest lake in New England (322 square miles), Champlain forms the New York—Vermont boundary. It stretches south from the Canadian border for 120 miles, varying from a quarter-mile to 12 miles wide. Once the Champlain Canal opened in 1823, large ships could sail from New York City to Montreal or the Great Lakes. Although Vermont is the only New England state without ocean frontage, we have over 430 other lakes and ponds, three major rivers, and 29 smaller, navigable rivers.

Lake Champlain contains one peninsula and a cluster of islands that form Grand Isle County. For two months late in the twentieth century, Champlain was known as the sixth Great Lake.

Ll

Champlain

L leads to long, lovely Lake Champlain,
blue water with islands forming a chain.
The largest lake that New England can claim
borrowed a French explorer's name.

Vermont produces more maple syrup than any other state. When a can or jug says "Vermont Maple Syrup," people know it's the best. Visitors come from all over the world to watch farmers turn sap into syrup.

Vermont's state tree, the sugar maple, can produce as much as ten gallons of sap every winter—but it takes between 20 and 40 gallons of sap to make one gallon of syrup.

Natives taught early settlers to collect the "sweet water" from maple trees and turn it into syrup by dropping hot stones into hollowed logs filled with the sap. Sugarmakers now boil away the sap's water in large evaporators heated by wood, stirring constantly. During syrup season, a mouth watering aroma fills the sugarhouses, and evaporators run constantly. The syrup must be kept fresh and cold or it will spoil, so sugarmakers work quickly.

Mmmm is for Maple syrup,
a yummy treat that farmers stir up.
In winter, they tap the sugar maple tree,
for sap to make maple syrup for you and me!

m M

Just as 50 states form our nation, many Native American tribes together formed the great Algonquin nation. In Vermont, the Abenaki, Penacook, and Mahican peoples roamed the forests until the powerful New York Iroquois drove them out. The Abenaki returned in the early 1600s and, with help from the French, eventually defeated the Iroquois.

We still use some Algonquin place names. "Winooski" means "wild onion." The Winooski River once passed through fields full of wild onions. The name for Lake Memphremagog is based on the Abenaki word meaning "beautiful waters." Do you know other places with Algonquin names?

N nods to Natives,
the first people on this land.
Algonquin tribes came here to live
in this wooded wonderland.

N
n

Orchard is our word for O.
Here you'll see apples grow.
First, blossoms bloom, pink, or white,
then apples ripen. Take a bite!

The apple is Vermont's state fruit. Almost every Vermont farm has an orchard filled with apple trees, and perhaps peach, plum, and pear trees, too. Vermont is one of our country's leading McIntosh producers.

Over the years farmers and scientists have developed more than 8,000 kinds of apples. They all bud with pink or white blossoms in the spring. Those flowers require pollen from another apple tree to produce fruit. A full-grown tree can yield up to 30 bushels of apples in a year. McIntosh apples are bright red and shiny, delicious for eating and for squeezing to make cider.

You can see orchards and cider mills throughout Vermont. Allenholm Farm, in South Hero, is Vermont's oldest commercial orchard.

P p

P is for President.
Two Vermonters were sent
as president to Washington, D.C.;
they ran our country expertly.

Born in Fairfield in 1829, Chester A. Arthur was a lawyer who became president when President James A. Garfield died in 1881. Our 21st president was an honest and hardworking man who helped reform the way people are chosen for government jobs. He left office in 1885 and died the next year. A replica of his house sits in Fairfield.

When President Warren G. Harding died in 1923, Vice President Calvin Coolidge was visiting his family's home in Plymouth Notch. By the light of a kerosene lamp, Mr. Coolidge was sworn into office as our 30th president by his father, who was a notary public. President Coolidge was known for his honesty and skill in business and foreign affairs. "Silent Cal" left Washington in 1928, never explaining why he decided not to run for another term. He died in 1933, at age 61. You can tour his home in Plymouth Notch.

A quarry is a deep, open hole where stone is cut, mined, or blasted out of the ground. Vermont is famous for its marble and granite quarries.

Marble is a hard rock with pretty patterns and colors. The first U.S. marble quarry opened in East Dorset in 1785. Proctor's marble quarries are among the world's largest. Proctor's streets are lined with marble sidewalks and marble buildings. The capitol building in Montpelier and other famous buildings in our country were built using Vermont marble.

Vermont quarries also mine granite, a strong rock with a grainy, even texture. Barre has been the granite center of the world for more than a century, mining white and blue-gray rock. The Supreme Court Building in Montpelier and the 24-foot-high Robert Burns Monument in Barre were built with Barre granite.

A very big hole that you can view,
Quarry begins with the letter Q.
Here, marble and granite can be found;
big blocks are cut right out of the ground.

Vermont's state flower, red clover is the food of choice for herds of Holstein cows and for the Vermont state insect, the honeybee. Early farmers brought this perennial plant from Europe to feed their herds and flocks in America.

Clover is important for feeding farm animals, moose, and deer, but it also nourishes the soil. Red clover is the most common type of clover. Growing between six and ten inches high, its purplish, rosy flower perches on a straight stem. Red clover nectar needs to be cross-fertilized, but it lies deep within the flower; bees are the only insects who can reach it.

R is for our flower, Red clover,
    a flower that honeybees hover over.
Red clover blossoms cluster in bunches,
    which cows like to munch for their sweet lunches.

S s

S salutes the Seal,
      symbol of our state.
        Its pictures reveal
            things that make Vermont great.

Vermont's great seal was designed in the midst of the American Revolution by an artist named Ira Allen. He included the symbols that represented Vermont 225 years ago; they still represent the things that make our state special today.

Designed as a circle, the seal says "Vermont" in the center; below that is our state motto, "Freedom & Unity." Wavy lines around the edge suggest the sky and water. A wheat sheaf stands in each of the four corners. Mountains and trees roll across the seal. A cow grazes beneath one lone pine tree that stands at the top center.

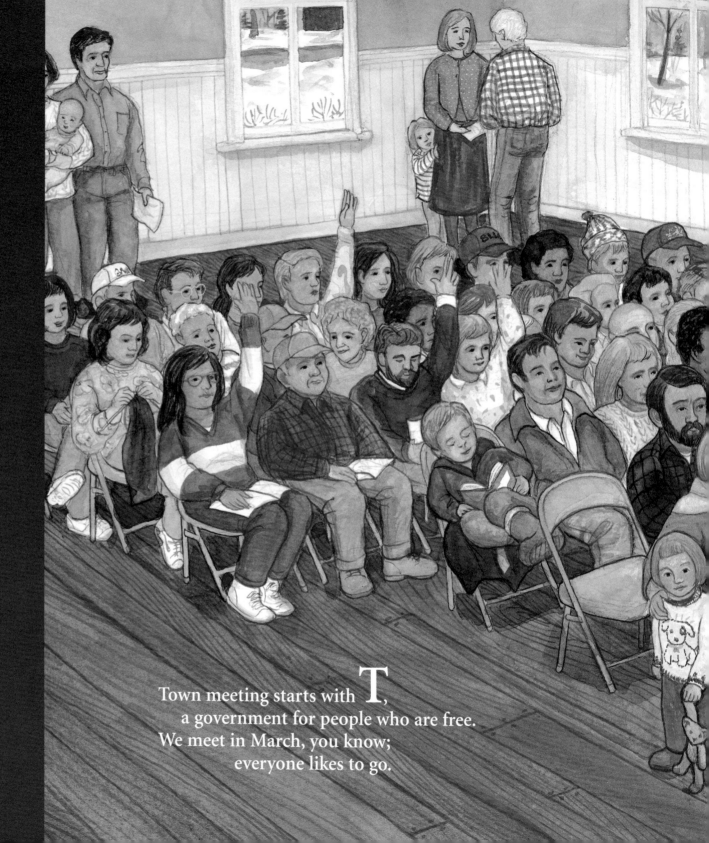

The town meeting is a democratic tra-
dition dating back to the earliest days
of our country. This is a form of government run by the people themselves.

In Vermont, the first Tuesday in March
is Town Meeting Day, a very important
date. The citizens of each town meet
in their town hall to elect officials, dis-
cuss improvements, approve budgets,
vote upon taxes, pass laws, and decide
on important matters. The town clerk
keeps records for the meetings.

T t

Town meeting starts with T,
    a government for people who are free.
We meet in March, you know;
    everyone likes to go.

Not all history happens on land. Lake Champlain has always been one of our nation's most important interior waterways; countless ships have sailed over its waters. During storms or disasters on decks through the ages, many ships—no one knows how many—sank. Underwater Vermont hides ships that date as far back as the 1700s.

The state of Vermont maintains five underwater historic sites for scuba divers: the General Butler, the Horse Ferry, the Phoenix, the Coal Barge, and the Diamond Island Stone Boat. Yellow buoys with guidelines lead the way down to the wrecks.

U u

And now we come to the letter U
and an interesting place that is hard to view.
Underwater Vermont hides treasures very old
in sunken ships and their cargo hold.

Less than one-third of all Vermonters live in the urban areas of Burlington, Bennington, Rutland, Essex, or Colchester. Most Vermonters live on farms or in villages. Most of our villages were settled in the colonial days and designed around a town green where cows and sheep would graze. Often, a church with a high, spiky steeple sits at the head of the green. Old colonial homes, a few shops, and perhaps a school or two border the town square. Farms and forests stretch beyond the borders of the villages.

Artists, photographers, and visitors love to paint, sculpt, photograph and write about the clean, serene beauty of Vermont's villages.

EAST CORINTH, VT.

POSTCARD

PLACE STAMP HERE

Miss Lucie Stein
Dalton Drive
Colchester, Vt

RIPTON, VT.

STOWE, VERMONT

Village starts with the letter **V**.
Visitors come to Vermont to see
pretty houses, town scenery,
old farms, Holsteins, and mountain greenery.

THIS SPACE MAY BE USED FOR MESSAGE   THIS SPACE FOR THE ADDRESS

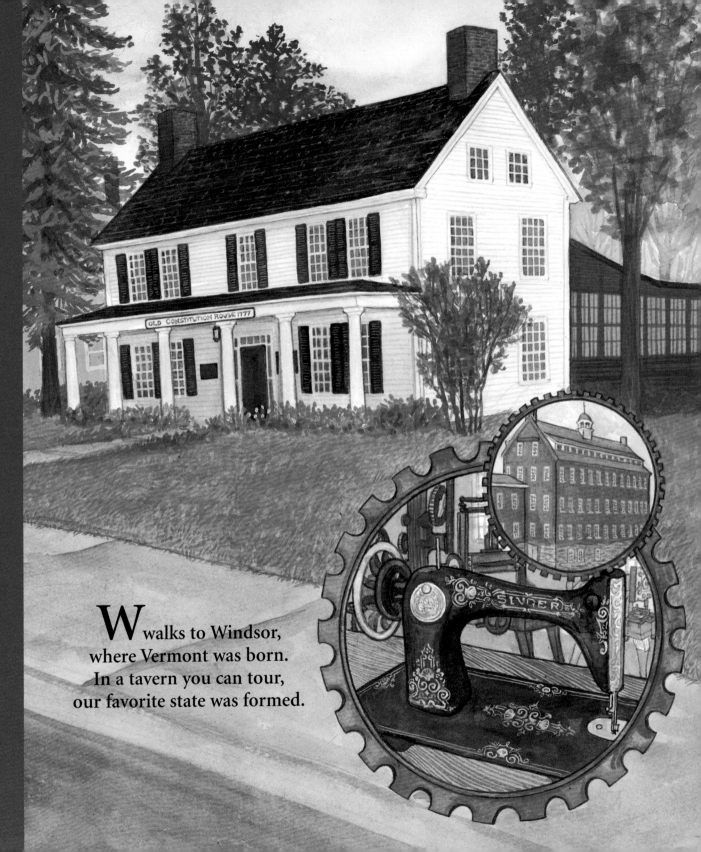

Exactly one year after the Declaration of Independence was signed, another new republic appeared on the North American continent: the Republic of Vermont. In July 1777, delegates gathered in a tavern in Windsor to draft the state's first constitution—and it was visionary. Those delegates prohibited slavery within Vermont's borders and established voting rights for all men. The Old Constitution House still stands.

Vermont's General Assembly met in Windsor until 1805. Later in the nineteenth century, Windsor became a center for inventors who worked on firearms, hydraulic pumps, coffee percolators, and the sewing machine. These and many more inventions can be seen in the American Precision Museum on Windsor's Main Street.

W walks to Windsor,
where Vermont was born.
In a tavern you can tour,
our favorite state was formed.

When Vermont is covered with a thick blanket of snow, Vermonters and visitors sled, tour the wintry countryside in sleighs or snowmobiles, build burly snowmen, ice skate on frozen ponds, and ski.

Vermont has more than 220 mountains, with 18 ski resorts. Killington, Jay Peak, and Burke Mountain offer some of the most challenging downhill ski trails anywhere. Vermont was also the first state to develop a network of cross-country ski trails. In 1968, Johannes von Trapp, of *The Sound of Music*'s von Trapp family, opened America's first cross-country ski center in Stowe. Here, cross-country trails, teachers, and equipment were offered at one location for the first time. Vermont now has more than 280 miles of groomed cross-country trails and many skiers create their own.

X looks like the tracks of skis
when skiers slip and cross their knees.
Skis appear when autumn flees,
snows blow, and temperatures freeze.

Y yells Yay! for Yankee,
  someone who is thrifty and shy,
    with a twinkle in the eye,
      and a sense of humor that is dry.

No one knows the origin of the word, but Vermonters all know what Yankee means. You've probably heard the phrases "shrewd as a Yankee" and "clever as a Yankee." Yankees had to be shrewd and clever to make a living in Vermont's harsh, cold climate.

Some dictionaries say that Yankee comes from the Scottish yankie, meaning a sharp, clever woman. Others believe it is an Indian pronunciation of French Anglais, which means English. Early Dutch setters were often called Jan Kees, short for the Dutch names Jan and Cornelis. In the early 1700s, Jonathan Hastings of Massachusetts was the first to use the word Yankee to mean excellence. A "Yankee good horse" was an excellent horse.

Before the American Revolution, the British used Yankee to poke fun at New Englanders, but after the war, we used the word proudly. A Vermont Yankee now means someone shy, short on words, with a humorous worldview and an economical way of living.

Z...z

Zerah Colburn starts with **Z**.
He multiplied numbers before he was three.
The world called Zerah a boy wonder.
He could solve math problems without a blunder.

Zerah Colburn was a mathematical genius who, even before he could read or write, could multiply two four-digit numbers in his head in seconds. Born in 1804, Zerah toured America and Europe as a little boy, dazzling audiences with his mathematical abilities. Later in life, he became a clergyman and professor of languages in Norwich.

$$275614 \times 892350$$

$$7928693 \times 8734526$$

Z

z

A Quarry Full of Vermont Facts

1. What is Vermont's state bird and what makes him special?

2. What phrase made Ethan Allen famous?

3. What is Vermont's special drink?

4. Who was one of our state's famous child wonders?

5. What is Vermont's official state animal? How did it get its name?

6. What city is Vermont's capital? What makes it special?

7. What are the three official rocks of Vermont? How are they used?

8. Why did Vermonters build covers on their bridges?

9. Who gave Vermont its name? What is Vermont's nickname?

10. What is our state tree? What treat does it give us?

11. What is our state motto?

12. What made our 1777 Constitution special?

13. Was Vermont one of the original Thirteen Colonies?

14. What makes Windsor special?

15. What is our official state cold-water fish? Warm-water fish?

16. What is a grossular garnet?

17. Is Lake Champlain the only Vermont lake? What makes it special?

28. How many Vermont-born-and-bred presidents were there? Who were they?

1. The hermit thrush is Vermont's state bird. Many birdwatchers believe that its song is the most musical of all North American birds.

2. When the Green Mountain Boys captured Fort Ticonderoga, Allen demanded the British surrender "in the name of the Great Jehovah and the Continental Congress."

3. Milk is our official state drink.

4. Zerah Colburn was a mathematical genius whose talent was recognized long before he could read or write.

5. The Morgan horse is Vermont's official state animal. The Morgan was named for Justin Morgan, who received the first colt as payment for a debt.

6. Montpelier has the lowest population of any United States capital city. Its capitol building is made of Vermont marble.

7. Marble and granite are very hard rocks used for building. Slate is gray-blue and splits into smooth layers. In the old days, it was often used for roofs and gravestones.

8. The roof protected the floor and structure of the bridge from decay, helping it last longer. Some people think that bridges were covered to keep the snow off, but actually Vermonters had to shovel snow onto the bridge floors so that sleighs could go across.

9. French explorer Samuel de Champlain saw our mountains covered with trees all colored in shades of green and wrote about "les vert mont," which is French for "The Green Mountains." Our nickname picks up on this origin: the Green Mountain State.

10. The sugar maple tree is Vermont's state tree. In the winter, farmers collect the sap that runs from the maple tree and boil it to give us maple syrup.

11. "Freedom and Unity" is our state motto.

12. It was the first constitution in the United States to outlaw slavery and allow all adult male citizens the right to vote.

13. No. In 1791, Vermont joined the United States as its 14th state.

14. Vermont's first state capitol, Windsor, was where our first constitution was written. Later, it became a center for inventors and inventions.

15. Vermont's official state cold-water fish is the brook trout and the state warm-water fish is the walleye pike.

16. The grossular garnet is Vermont's state gem. It is a crystallized mineral composed of silica, aluminum, and magnesium.

17. Lake Champlain is one of more than 430 lakes in Vermont, and it is the largest. Ships can sail from Lake Champlain down to the Atlantic Ocean.

18. Two U.S. presidents hailed from Vermont: Chester A. Arthur (21st president) and Calvin Coolidge (30th president).

Cynthia Furlong Reynolds

As a child, Cynthia Furlong Reynold's grandmother asked her to write a story, and while young Cynthia protested that she didn't even know her letters yet, her grandmother insisted she write something down. Later that day, her grandmother turned her scribbles into a wonderful adventure of a little girl just like Cynthia.

Cynthia has written for newspapers and publications across the country. She is the author of *L is for Lobster: A Maine Alphabet*; *H is for Hoosier: An Indiana Alphabet*; and *S is for Star: A Christmas Alphabet*.

She lives with her husband, Mark, and their three children outside Ann Arbor, Michigan.

Ginny Joyner

Ginny Joyner began her career as an artist at a very early age, decorating her parents' furniture and walls with her lively creations. She was told that paper was a more acceptable surface, and since then, people have enjoyed her work very much.

She graduated in 1986 from the Rhode Island School of Design, and has been working as a freelance illustrator in Vermont for 12 years. She still paints an occasional table or wall, and is honored to call *M is for Maple Syrup* her first children's book. She lives in Colchester, Vermont, where she has a studio and lives with her amazing daughter, Lucie.